Note To Self
Poetry That Helps

M. D. Raine

Time
Confidence
Self
Love
Dreams
Spiritual

Table of Contents

able of Contents (Continued)

Note To Self

Don't forget
yourself.
Don't regret
feelings felt.
Devote
more time,
note to self.
Love
every day.
Thinking of
words to say.
Nothing else is guaranteed
to stay.
Note to self,
you'll be ok.
Not all is lost
at any cost.
It's not all your fault.
Don't be afraid to ask for
help,
note to self.
Stand proud,
but not too loud.
Be humble without
making a sound.
Time will tell
and actions will yell,
note to self.
Don't fear
that which isn't clear.
We don't know when
the end is near.
Above all else,
that which matters most

is that you're here,
note to self.
Mirrors don't reflect
truth.
Only the heart will respect
you
when you want to be someone else,
note to self.
Nothing's wrong with solitude
as long as you look within you.
Don't worry about anything else,
note to self.
Precious is the time
we have.
Lost is the time
we had.
A no win situation
that seems sad,
but above all else
enjoy what's given.
Note to self,
start living.
Never forget
who you are.
Never regret
what you'll become.
Above all else
be someone,
note to self.
When all falls apart,
when you break my heart.
When the cards are dealt
and in hand,
note to self,
you're my only friend.

Time

All is connected,
all part of one.
Rhythm is reflected
and in sync.
Yourself, neglected
and about to break.

Swallowed

I must meet my deadline.
Consumed by the poison
known as time,
running out
is a hard pill
to swallow.
Join the competition.
Join the blind.
Repetition
will follow,
entrapment
for the mind.
Both ends burned
will eventually meet,
not concerned
with me.
It's a hard pill
to swallow.
A long climb uphill
towards tomorrow.
It's a race
not yet won.
Make haste
and start to run.
It's a hard pill
to swallow.
Why can't it wait
until tomorrow?

Seams

Time is money,
give or take.
Time is greedy,
live or break.
You have to look for the cracks,
small spaces between.
With sanity still intact
and your plate clean.
Keep it together,
no time to break.
It will get better,
make no mistake.
To and fro,
pendulum swing.
Places to go,
all part of a scheme.
Stitched together
by the thread of time.
It will get better,
never mind
the lose seams.
Chaos pours through,
loss is nothing new.
Holding it together
is the best you can do.

Hand In Hand

Around the fortress
of rhythm,
the mistress
of the unforgiving
extends her hand.
All while
counting down your
time of living
in this land.
You can embrace
her touch,
hand in hand.
Face
the rush
of demand.
Go with the flow
as she extends her reach.
Everywhere you go,
harsh lessons she has to teach.
Hand in hand,
don't lose touch.
She has a plan
for all of us.

Expense

How much would it cost
if I spent time on me?
What would be lost
for my tired self to be free?
What could be done
today
can wait for another sun
to rise tomorrow.
At what expense
can someone
borrow
to be free.
I would give
all my burdens away
to live.
Just one more day
to forgive.
At what expense
does it cost
for precious time lost?

M. D. Raine

Solitude

I sit and wait
patiently
for whatever fate
awaits me.
I show gratitude,
even with all that I've
been through.
Just stepping stones,
mile markers
for time spent alone.
Lost in thought,
I feel at peace.
Solitude brought
me
closer to myself
than I'll
ever
be.

In Time

Like clockwork,
tiny gears working in rhythm,
to and fro,
we are given
more time than you know
to start living.
No need to rush,
no need for hurry.
No need to push,
no need to worry.
In time
all is done.
Nothing left behind.
It has just begun.
In time
all is one.
You will find
that eventually
it will be
done.

Confidence

Stand to make a difference.
Stand to be free.
I wish I had confidence
in just being me.

Shadow of a Doubt

Shadow of a doubt
is a battle within
to be without.
It follows you
in the light of day
and even in the dark of night.
Shadow of a doubt
follows me
throughout
even in the light of day
and dark of night
I can't go without.
It always remains in sight.
Shadow of a doubt,
I can't win the fight.
I can't go without
doubt.

M. D. Raine

The Mask

Two extremes
you face.
Just a few schemes
to help you find your place.
Show no fear
just keep a steady pace.
Wear this mask,
whether it's real or fake
to hide your face.
Put on a smile
even if it's just for a while.
Show no fear.
Show no denial.
The truth
is left behind.
All that remains
is the fruit
of the blind.
So wear this mask,
hide your face.
Carry on with the task
to find your place.
What if I show
my face?
What if I get to know
my real place?
All emotion
shown on my face.
So I remove the mask
and face the hate.
A task
I
must undertake.

Consequences

Should I let my demons
come out and play?
They keep my emotions
at bay.
Things I'd love to do,
things I'd love to say,
the answer's always,
"nope, not today."
They argue
that there's consequences.
They demand
that I put up my defenses.
They put me at constant alert.
It's constant fear.
You will be hurt
even if you think
that the coast is clear.
I want to be free,
even if only for a day.
I just want to be ok.

M. D. Raine

Your Friend

Hello,
nice to meet you.
Time you get to know
me.
I'm everything
you'd like to be.
Every dream
only your eyes
see.
I'm a friend
who will lend you
my hand
and get you
on your feet.
Come on
we can make a difference,
you and I.
No need to feel alone.
I'm your confidence.
I'm the sky.
Reach for me
and take my hand.
You will see
that you can stand.
One step at a time.
Small in might.
Soon you will find
the will to fight.
I will never leave
your side.
You must believe
that everything
will be
alright.

Enough

When times get tough
and there's too much
stuff
to be done,
I stop and stand
in place
just so I can
think.
I've had enough.
I'm about to break.
It's too much
for me to take.
I can get through
this,
make no mistake.
I've had enough
today.
I need a break.
So stop and stand
in place.
Make a demand.
Make your case
that enough is enough
today.

M. D. Raine

Reflect

I fear my reflection,
oh how it haunts me so.
I fear rejection.
Some places I will
not go.
How could I fear
what I see?
Soon
it will be what
I saw
taunting me.
It's the truths
hidden
that bear fruit
that's forbidden
unless you dare
to take the first bite.
Beauty is within
reflected
throughout.
It's what you're
given.
It's what
you can live
without.
First
you must see.
Open your eyes.
It will hurt
to be free.
Find your worth
and reflect
back
for all to
see.

Love

Give and take,
live to make
all of
your heart's content.
Love
until
your last breath
is spent.

M. D. Raine

Fragile

Fragile
is your soul.
Mind of a child,
heart of gold.
I've walked miles upon miles
and the same stories
I have told.
You're only young
once.
So be bold,
stand strong.
Break the mold
just as long
as you handle with care
for life is fragile
and not fair.

Love Note

To whom it may concern,
To you who has not yet
learned,
you could give
all your love away.
You could live
with words you
couldn't say.
As long as there
is still today
I love
you more
than words I could say.
There is hope
in you.
So here's a note
for you.
A reminder
to stay true.
There's no greater love
than the love
for
you!

Shell

I've put up my defenses.
I've built a wall.
I've made choices
that affect us all.
A bitter hell
I'm trapped behind.
A story to tell
in due time.
I feel
more than you know.
It's real,
trapped behind
a shell.
What's out
isn't in.
What's in
is hell.

Sacrifice

You live to give
a little everyday.
You live to watch
it all be taken
away.
It's a push
and pull.
A constant rush
for us all.
It's give
and take.
You either live
or you break.
It's a sacrifice
you make.
It's the friction
of life.
In action
you don't think twice.
In time
you understand the
sacrifice.

Gifts

You have a lot to offer.
Don't let them tell you otherwise.
You have a lot to give.
Open up their eyes.
Show them a different
point of view.
Show them a different
side of you.
Give them something
to help in the darkest
of nights.
Give them something
to keep them going
in the fight.
Bring hope.
Bring peace.
Give something
to help cope
and put their mind at
ease.
Help them to remember
a better time.
Help each other
find
their gifts.

Two Halves of a Heart

If you can find it within
yourself
to be forgiving
to everyone else,
then that's
love.
If you can find it within
yourself
to believe
in everyone else,
then that's
love.
If you can find
both within
yourself,
then that's
love.

Dreams

I love to wonder,
and I wonder what it is to love.
There's nothing more that
I dream of.

Small Steps

I climbed the stairs
today.
That's enough for me.
You can't compare,
so you say.
I got out of bed
today.
That's enough for me.
To some
small steps
are a victory,
a feat well won.
I will win.
I will be accepted
because in the end
expect the unexpected.

Try

Let's build something,
you and I.
We can do anything
if we try.
You might fail
or you could fly.
It's do
or die
never knowing
what can be accomplished.
Time is flying by
so get going
and give it a try.

The Promise

You know what I see?
A whole world
of possibilities
in little 'ol
me.
You know what I know?
The ocean is deep
and mountains are high.
I'll keep
looking up in the sky
and wonder
why?
Fields are green
and the world is wide.
I'll still dream
until I die.

Give

Lines cross your face,
a path leading to an
unknown place.
What once was
withers.
What now is,
I must consider
the only options
I have left.
As time has shown
I find that I have grown.
Things I love,
now gone.
Things I've learned,
I must pass on.
I dare
not regret
until my last breath.
I lived
doing that which I loved.
I give
you all that I dreamed of.

Gone

Paint the picture.
Write the story,
and sing the song.
Become a fixture
in people's hearts
before you're gone.
Take the test.
Study hard
and become strong.
Give it your best
before you're gone.
Plant the seed.
Watch it grow
and succeed.
Set yourself free
before you're gone.

Spiritual

What I believe,
is held in heart.
What I see
is far from truth.
So, I believe
in me,
and so should
you.

Stasis

Many places
I have been.
Many faces
I have seen.
All make an imprint
within me.
They all make
such a beautiful
memory.
I've learned.
I've listened.
Now it's my turn
to be
enlightened.
So I stop
and take a deep breath.
Ease my mind
as I stand in stasis.
I unwind
and remember these
places.
I stop time
just to escape
within.
Find faith
within.
In the deep sea
of thought,
I'll find me
before I'm caught
in
stasis.

M. D. Raine

Lift Me Up

I've been dragged through
the dirt.
I've been kicked around
until it hurt.
Through the scars, blood, sweat
and tears
take a stand for who you are
and show no fear.
Stand for your worth.
Stand for love.
Stand when it hurts.
If you're above,
lift me up
when I'm not strong enough.
To those above,
when you look down
extend your grasp.
Lift me up!
It's all that I ask.
Don't kick me further
below
in the dark unknown.
Lift me up
and make me strong.
Take hold of my hand
before I'm too far gone.
Lift me up,
and I'll do the same for my fellow man.
Lift me up
before I'm gone.
Sometimes you can't
stand on your own
so,
lift me up!

Emotional Sickness

I feel nothing,
as if I'm stone.
I wish everything
would leave me alone.
It's not that I don't care.
You think that I'm not there,
but I'm everywhere.
I feel
that I'm pulled in every direction
all at once.
Scattered
in depression
that dare
not show.
I still care,
just so you know.
I'm everywhere..
I'm here.
I'm there.
Show no fear.
I don't care,
but I do
more than you know.
So what do I fear?
It's what I can't show.
I'll lock it up
in a deep, dark place
until it overflows.
I don't feel
so well,
but you'll never know.
You can say I don't
care,
but that's not fair.

Don't judge what you can't see
trapped within me.
I just don't know
how to show
and that's what
sickens
me.

The Pearl

Take your time.
No need to rush.
Ease your mind.
Make it hush.
Take it with a grain
of salt
or sand.
It's all the same
under pressure.
When things
get tough
take your time.
You're not yet
a diamond
in the rough.
Ease your mind
and you will find
all things work out
in time.

Centered

Draw a circle
in the middle of the floor.
Take your place
in the center
and sit.
Don't worry about anything
anymore.
No one can enter
and no regrets.
When you are centered
nothing and no one
can enter.
Keep your circle small,
but stand tall
and centered.
They'll come knocking,
but none shall enter.
Put your mind at ease
and keep blocking.
Stay centered.

Within, Without

If you stay in,
you'll miss out.
If you go out,
you'll be in.
It's a constant war,
a silent conqueror of my mind.
I don't want to fight anymore.
I don't want to remain blind.
Some might find
that within
it's better to do without.
You don't have to fit in.
That's not what it's all about.
So I'll go within,
you stay out.
Sometimes it's better
to be
without.

Worth

You're worth more than the shirt
on your back.
You're worth more than the dirt
they toss at
you.
Stand and fight.
It's their loss
and they should pay the price.
Pennies to riches,
it's not how much
determines one's worth.
It's what's within
even when you're down
in the dirt.
Your soul
is worth more
than all the gold.
Your worth
is measured in strength,
covered in dirt.
You'll rise above
with love
and that's my
belief.

Afraid of the Dark

I'm afraid of the dark,
the unknown parts
of the heart.
Don't turn out the light.
I fear the unseen
mysteries of the
night.
My demons
might
come out
and play,
only to be suppressed
by the light
of day.
I'm afraid of the dark,
the deepest depths
of the heart
unseen by the light
of day.
Don't turn out the light
because I'm afraid of the dark.
I can't win this fight
in the deepest depths of my
heart.

M. D. Raine

Matters of the Heart

Don't get me started
about matters of the heart.
We all feel defeated
right from the start.
Don't give up
when you feel stuck.
You must play your part,
win or lose,
matters of the heart.
You must choose.
So many paths
that are split in two.
You feel
so confused.
So don't get me started
about matters of the heart.
I feel defeated
in thought.
I feel lost
and caught.
Don't get me started
about matters of the heart.
My spirit depleted
right from the start.
I feel defeated
with a broken heart.

Stepping Stones

You're either with me
or in my way.
Just another stepping stone,
either way.
There's a lesson
to be learned
from everyone who crosses
your path.
Good or bad,
we cut our losses
and nothing lasts.
Sometimes you must walk
alone.
Watch your step
and don't trip
over stones.
The journey is rocky,
and the journey is steep.
The stepping stones
keep me on my
feet.

Blind

How can I be
that which I'm not.
I simply can not see,
my own fault.
Strength within
remains hidden
until called upon.
How can I find
that which I've lost.
All the time
at my exhaust.
Treasure lies between.
A measure of the unseen.
Open your eyes.
All is not lost.
There are no goodbyes.
All that you thought
wasn't there,
is.

Tomorrow

I've been here before.
Lost and my heart
torn.
The return is inevitable.
What I've learned is irreversible.
The winding path
is full of sorrow,
that's for certain.
But it won't last.
Look for tomorrow
behind the curtain.
Raise it high
for this isn't the end.
You must fight
and defend.
You deserve
tomorrow.
It can't be reserved.
It can't be borrowed.
It must be fought for
through joy and sorrow.
Though not promised,
you can fight to achieve this.
It might be hit.
It might be missed,
but never forget,
you got this!

M. D. Raine

The River's Edge

Come sit by the calm waters
lost in thought and frivolous matters.
Soothe your soul
at the river's edge,
as the sun's gold
dances on calm waters.
Be still
and the heart will follow.
You will feel
small, though
moved by calm waters.
There's no hurry here.
There's no race.
The waters are clear.
This is the place
to hit
reset.

Real(ize)

As I've grown old(er),
eyes who's sight
is hindered,
I grow bolder
as I remember
those who are still here
and those long past.
Everything becomes more clear,
nothing lasts.
Those who remain
beside me
are real.
Still the same,
but different is how
I feel.
Fight the fake.
Forge yourself in stone.
Learn from a mistake
even if you learn alone.
Your heart will shield
you from the lies.
You must do your part and
build.
Follow your heart
and
realize.

M. D. Raine

Just A Reminder

You are but one,
unique and whole.
You are but one,
your actions speak
for your soul.
You are but one,
but love like no other.
You are but one,
extend your hand to many.
You are but one,
make time for yourself
plenty.
You are but one,
no need to rush.
You are but one,
no need to push.
You are one,
like no one else.
You are one,
love yourself!

www.ingramcontent.com/pod-product-compliance
Lightning Source LLC
Chambersburg PA
CBHW032132050726
47590CB00008B/3054